Reflective Journal

Talethia O. Edwards

ISBN: 979-8-9874492-4-0

For information about custom editions, special sales, premium and bulk purchases, please contact:
Talethia Edwards
www.talethiaedwards.com

First Edition
Printed in the U.S.A

Dedication & Acknowledgements

This book is dedicated to Bishop Harold W. Edwards, II my husband, Big daddy. Thanks for loving me and always showing up.

To my children Jermaine, Haniah, Elijah, Joshua, Haleigh, Harper, Harley and Raymond: You all taught me deep love, you taught me how to explore myself and evolve.

To my sister Anita who has been my prayer partner and accountability partner through the process. Thank you

And to my village you all know who you are. God has placed us together to not just be friends but we are family. My life is rich because of every one of you.

Thank you to all the pushers in my life, I would be nowhere without the love, belief and encouragement. you all have poured into me over the years..

A Letter From The Authors Pen

This book is an act of obedience. Many people live their entire life not being obedient to the call on their lives, and honestly, it's taken me years to actually begin this process. I think it was fear that was holding me back. Sharing myself and my words with the world seemed so invasive. While most people feel very close to me, I have always been a private person. Not really wanting to go into the most intimate pieces about myself. But what I understand about this book is that once I finish it, it will unlock everything that this act has been holding up.

It's taken some time, but I realize that in my life, not everything is about me. Most of it is about seeing If I am trustworthy enough to do what is required so that people behind me can reap the blessing. That sounds worse than what it really is. See, when you trust and believe God, you must know that what you think he has for you is always miniature compared to what he really has in store.

Writing has always been a kind of release for me, and it's difficult to believe that I struggled to find the words to write this book. Some people know long before their first book that they were created to write. I cannot quite say that I am one of those people, but I can say that I have always been a writer. It's what I do to understand situations, moments myself, and frankly the world. I love words, I love them even more on paper. With eight children, I cannot say that I am able to read or write as much as I used to, but my lack of writing time has never changed what writing and words have done for me.

A Letter From The Authors Pen

This book was compiled at a turbulent time in my life. Things were rocky and unsure. However, I believe this is when God does his most perfect work; in the places where we cannot trust ourselves and all we can do is trust him. I am at that place. I want to trust God with all the insecurities, doubts and imposter syndrome and see what is on the other side of obedience. I have so many questions, and so many reasons to not move forward, but I am doing it. I am going to move forward and look back all at the same time. I am going to revisit some old journals and include entries from periods in my life, and I am going to share new experiences.

So here it goes... enjoy my vulnerability through these pages, laugh at my immaturity and pray for me as I walk into the next phase of my life... journey with me.

- Talethia D. Edwards

Only Paper Understands

How to use this Journal

All of my life I can remember writing on scratch sheets of paper, or jotting down notes in the margins of my papers. I Wrote when I was imagining, goal setting and just capturing what was running through my head. This reflective journal is a combination of all of those things. I invite you into my life, my head and my heart as I share intimate moments and thoughts that I entrusted to paper. I invite you to read the entries I share, follow the prompts provided or just write what comes to mind as you sit with yourself and the thoughts that arise from what you read.

I figured that this book would never be finished if I didn't get started. My ramblings and thoughts in print, who would have thought? Surely not me. I started writing in a journal at a young age. It was just a way to vent and not have anyone tell me I was wrong for the way I feel. It has taken me two years to complete this project since I started, because I couldn't imagine how my journals could be interesting to anyone besides me. I am learning that we don't always have to know, we just have to do. When you write, try to be fully present in the moment and don't worry about how long it takes to finish an entry. Like me, you may pick it up and put it down several times before you move to the next page. That's perfectly fine because your reflections are all about you.

My journals aren't in date order like the Diary of Anne Frank but rather random since I never kept just one journal at any given time. I've always had multiple journals and I named them different things based on the time frame in my life so you will read entries from My Book of Life, Progress, Me, Myself & I, Famu Experience, A Mother's Heart, Misunderstood Mrs, and many more. If no one has ever done so before, I give you permission to be random. You don't have to be put together or proper here. Write from your current moment, thought and feeling. Allow yourself the grace to get lost in the paper, be honest and transparent with yourself and with God. This reflective journal is a space to journey the anger, the hurt, the happiness, the hope, the enjoyment, the anticipation.There is no right or wrong way to use this journal, don't think hard about it. Get lost in the pages because, truly, only paper understands!

Only Paper Understands

Writing serves a different purpose for everyone, for me it was a way to escape, a way to cope and a way to release.
Paper never seems to get offended at what I have to say.
Paper never asks me to repeat myself or reword what I said so it doesn't sound so harsh.
Paper accepts all my brutality and doesn't take advantage of my vulnerability.
It has served as my confidant, my counselor and my voice of reason.
When a thousand things are going on in my mind, and none of them make sense, the paper has never said, " Hold up, focus, I can't keep up."
All my life, paper has allowed me to be me, just who I am, never pretentious or shy.
Who I am, and all that I am,
only paper understands.

“

...enjoy my vulnerability through these pages, laugh at my immaturity and pray for me as I walk into the next phase of my life journey with me...

”

Dream Again

When I was younger, I dreamed all the time. I never had much of an imagination but as a child, I would make these wonderful collages of beautiful pictures from magazines that reflected the kind of family I wanted, the career I wanted to have, the places I wanted to travel and the house I wanted to live in. I dreamed out loud and in color because I didn't see those things in front of me. Not only did I not see them in front of me, but I also wasn't talking about them. Those magazine pages gave me an image of what was possible. They gave me the ability to dream things that had no model.

Dreaming can sometimes be difficult when you are trying to maintain and manage life. Sometimes life and trauma get so heavy that we lose our ability to dream.

I am understand this all to well and invite you to dream again!

Think about the dreams you have dreamed and the dreams you are still dreaming. Wake them up and give them life on these pages! What is the wildest dream you have that you haven't dared to speak out?

“

…I dreamed out loud and in color because I didn't see those things in front of me…

”

Date_____/_____/_____

A Mother's Heart

Every mother's dream is to have a daughter, one she can dress up, place little bows in her hair and parade her around for all to see.

God gave me just that, a daughter that filled my heart with pure joy. So adorable that her father couldn't call her anything but "wonderful." I remember all of her firsts; first smile, first tooth, first day of school. Now she is moving on past our first things together, into some firsts of her own.

Always in a mother's heart are thoughts of, "Will I be a good mother?", or, "Have I equipped you with all that's needed to be successful?". "Did I love you or discipline you enough?"

Then I look at her and my heart is so overwhelmed at the woman she has become.

Haniah, you are a mother's dream come true.

I love you, and I'm so proud of you!

From The Authors Pen

I am considered by many as the mother of mothers, but the truth of the matter is that I never wanted children. I was afraid of being responsible for anyone other than myself, as I had grown up the oldest of three children and much of that felt like pressure to me, and so I had resolved that I would not bring children into the world.

However, when that mindset eventually changed, I just knew I would be a boy mom, before I knew a boy mom was a thing. I never imagined I was equipped or soft enough to be a mother to daughters so I figured God would surely only give me sons.

However, God saw fit to bless me with a spunky little ball of fire in my first daughter. I am now the proud mother of four sons and four little girls, but I view all of my growth as a mother and as a person through the lens of Haniah. Since her birth she has taught me so many lessons about myself. I was made aware of my own fears and emotional trauma. I realized that I had worried so much about making them tough and preparing them for the world that I forgot to share the tenderness that would allow a person to leave a baby on our doorstep. Haniah has taught me that a mothers best intentions can still injure their children. I have learned so much from here and Honestly, they all have taught me different things, but I mark my emotional maturity with the birth of Haniah, she was the one I experienced all the girl mom firsts; the one I learn the hard lessons with, and get to perfect it with the other girls. She taught me that living boldly isn't an option but a mandate.

If you are a parent, what is your heart's desire for your children? Or What did you learn from your parents about parenting? If you are a parent what have you learned about yourself as you have parented your children?

“

...living boldly isn't an option but a mandate!

”

Date_____/_____/_____

Lessons From My Grandmother

This portion of the book cannot be found in any of my journals because I carry it in my heart. Anyone who knows me knows that my grandmother has been, and is even in death the person I cherish the most. Now my grandaddy Mr. Bubba is my heart, but he knows that Ms. Rose is the love of my life.

I learned so much about life and how to treat people from my grandmother. I feel like God cheated me by only giving her to me for ten years of my life, but those times were rich. Even as I write these words, I can hear my grandma saying to me "Say what you have to say, it doesn't matter what people think." That makes me smile. Those were good times.

As I think about the late night runs to Wendy's for a bacon and cheese baked potato for her and a frosty for me, or the 4am movie, I often got a chance to watch with her. The trips to the grocery store and her telling me not to ask for anything. And of course, I still asked. I could go on and on because there are so many memories and lessons I learned from my grandma.

From The Authors Pen

I am the whole of so much investment in my life, along the way people have come and gone and have shaped and inspired me in a way that has been lasting, but I get the question often, how did you get this way?

Where does this part of you come from? And when I think back most of it is from my grandmother. I don't know much about her childhood or her early life, but I learned from her silently. I watched how she showed up in the world, how she loved and how she opened her doors to people. I watched her keep her word and never back down on what she felt, I watched her keep her cool when all around her seemed to be falling apart. She had fun and entertained, she cooked and took rides with her sisters. She was cool before we knew the word. But she was also gone too soon. I lost my grandmother when I was ten years old. I felt like my world had shattered, like God had done me some injustice. It felt cruel to live a boisterous little girl in a world without the one person she was sure that loved her, that accepted her.

While I have had years to contend with God about his decision, what I hold on to is that fact that I know this lady loved me with her whole entire heart and that she would still be encouraging me to be exactly who I am, and say what I need to say. Her lessons, while silent, will always stick with me.

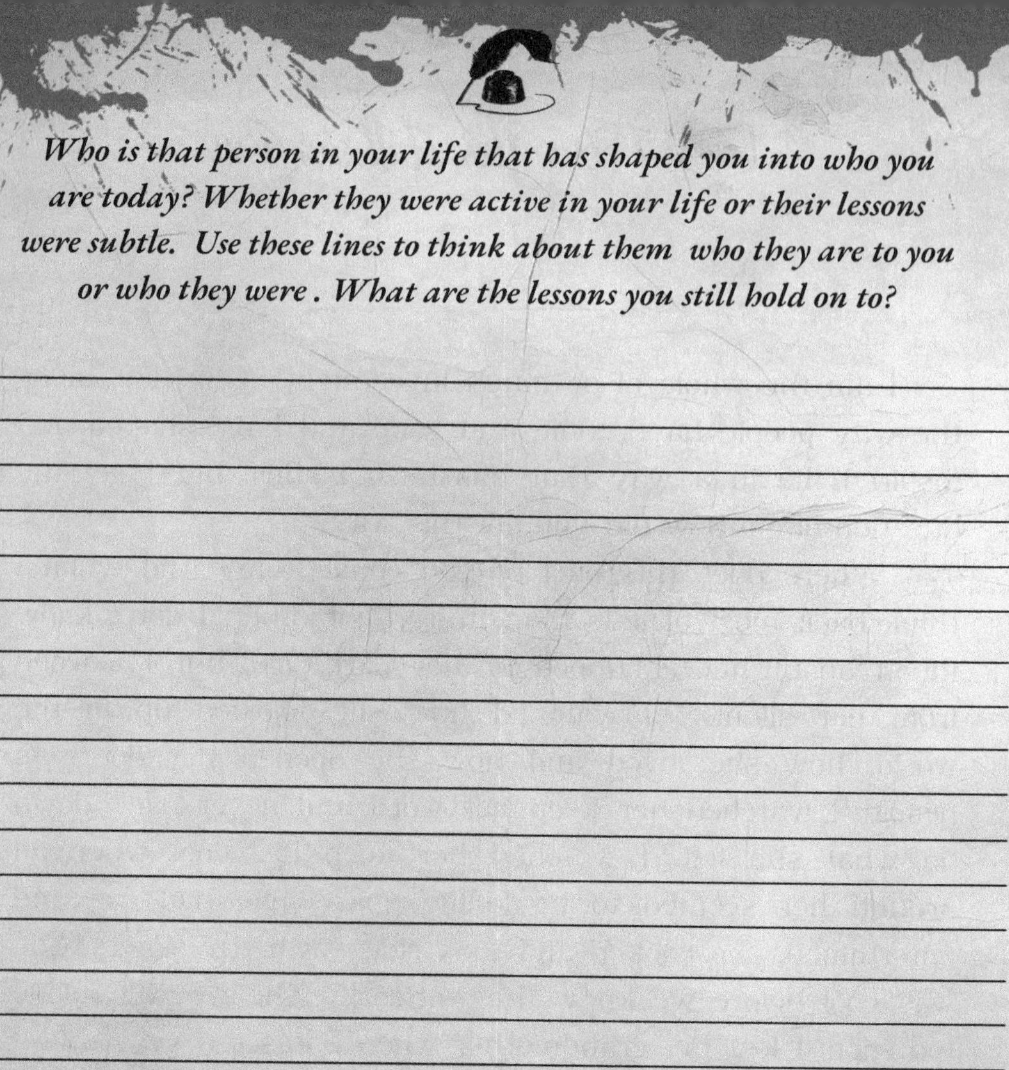

Who is that person in your life that has shaped you into who you are today? Whether they were active in your life or their lessons were subtle. Use these lines to think about them who they are to you or who they were . What are the lessons you still hold on to?

"

Say what you have to say, it doesn't matter what people think.

"

Date____/____/____

The Little Girl Inside

Why does this burn coming out?
Why can I feel tears?
I want to run from them, and I want to push them away, but at the same time I want to lean into them.
This pain I have isn't pain for the children that I bore and am raising, but for the little girl inside me.
It's for the little Talethia that learned in order to survive she had to be strong, and suck it up or pull herself together.
That little girl that still longed to be held and embraced or listened to fully.
The little girl inside the grown woman who still needed her mother, but struggled to find her comfort when it was needed the most.
The little girl that learned how to press down what she really felt because no one really cared about what she had going on inside.
The little girl that fell in love with paper.

From The Authors Pen

As you now know, I am the mother of eight wonderful children and I have to admit that it has been both my greatest sacrifice and my most rewarding journey.

I took all the precautions to learn how they were growing inside me, how their brains worked, what their cries sounded like, but what I hadn't bargained for was what I would soon learn about myself on this road to rearing this amazing group of humans. I wasn't prepared to face my own trauma head on, I wasn't prepared to challenge my socialization and the cultural norms I'd been taught. I wasn't prepared to love them so intensely despite the stages of life they were in sometimes. I wasn't prepared for what raising kids with another person meant, and how much effort it took to not jack them all up.

Parenting my kids taught me grace, it taught prayer, it taught me how to look at myself and fully heal if I wanted them to be whole.

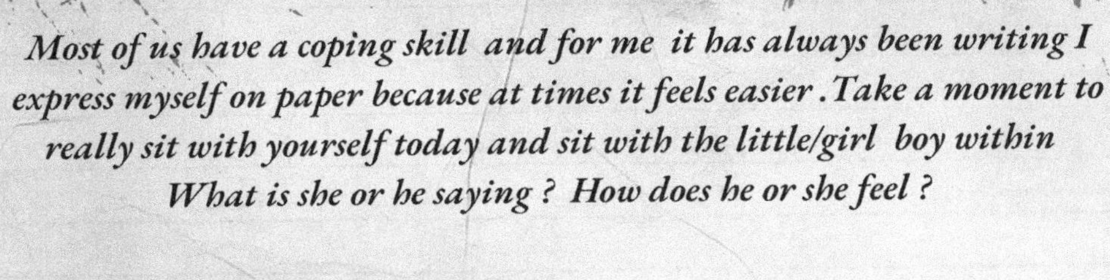

Most of us have a coping skill and for me it has always been writing I express myself on paper because at times it feels easier .Take a moment to really sit with yourself today and sit with the little/girl boy within What is she or he saying ? How does he or she feel ?

"Parenting my kids taught me grace, it taught prayer, it taught me how to look at myself and fully heal if I wanted them to be whole."

Date____/____/____

All Of Me

Poured out and emptied, This is how I feel.
I have given all of myself to everyone,
and there is nothing left.
They exclaim, "Talethia!" and there I am.
My husband, children, church, family and friends.

Feelings of loneliness and isolation fill me, despite there being so many people around.
I can't help but feel that I have given all of me.
All of me, with nothing in return.

I am always available and always working to make things happen. So often overlooked and under appreciated. No vacation because the family will die.
"What will we do without you? You know I need you. My life wouldn't be the same without you."
I AM ALL OUT OF ME

From The Authors Pen

There was a time in my life where other people controlled my time. I knew of boundaries, but dared to set some for myself. Sure, most of those people were the tiny little army I created, but nevertheless I was worn out and tired. I spent ten years of my life: pregnant, nursing and taking care of a family. Everyone was demanding things I did not have. Time, energy , wisdom, space. I needed things for myself, but it was too difficult to find them when everyone else had to come first.

As much as I am a communicator, at the time, I was unable to communicate what I needed. I didn't have the words or the strength to set the boundaries I needed to be well, to get rest or to take it. I was sad and a bit defeated that the life I'd chosen wasn't fulfilling me. I was a bit resentful of my husband and the wonderful children I was sacrificing everything for because I hadn't yet learned how to set boundaries. I hadn't learned how to take the time to care for myself. Truth is there were days when I actually wanted to walk off in the sunset and not return. I believed I had created enough of an infrastructure that things would flow smoothly without me.

One day looking in the mirror, I saw myself and didn't recognize the reflection looking back at me. I saw a reflection, but an emptiness occupied the space, and so I decided at that moment to choose what I needed for myself, which was peace and rest. I learned how to make space for what I needed, and take the time to invest the energy I was giving out into what would breathe life inside of me. See, the truth is that I wanted myself back. I wanted to know myself, to be able to hear myself think or accomplish the things I had thought of or wanted long before the little army I had created took over. I did that and it felt good.

Are you feeling like you have given all of yourself and have nothing left to give or maybe that used to be you?

Think about these words and write down some words of advice or encouragement to yourself or someone that may be feeling overwhelmed or unseen.

“

One day looking in the mirror, I saw myself and didn't recognize the reflection looking back at me. I saw a reflection, but an emptiness occupied the space, and so I decided at that moment to choose what I needed for myself...

”

Date____/____/____

Lost Love

I am in a whole new world when I am writing or creating, there are no right or wrongs here. Just saying and being and doing what feels right, what feels natural.

I had given over to my busy life and I wasn't writing as much as I would like; some scattered entries here and there, but not the consistent pen to paper and feeling the release in a way I had done so many times. I was missing it, I was full and these words wanted to escape. I had to get them out or I would burst, when I talk I have to say things just right, I have to make sure I don't get canceled by the culture. But this love affair with the paper was something that I missed that I needed and honestly it needs me.

So I am here writing again. trying to rekindle a lost place and a lost love...

As I went through my journals there were many entries that I found where the entries were incomplete, or half written. Many times I expressed the want and desire to write again, to go back to the first love I once shared with paper and words. This entry is not different I am mourning and grieving that I am not writing as much as I would like, and it expresses the fullness that I fell because I have neglected that love. Truth be told this entry was the last entry in the journal it was pulled from for over a year. So, while I was looking for that lost love I was consumed with life and did not always have the time or words to express.

What do you love but seem to have lost touch with?
Write about your long lost love .

"

I am in a
whole new world
when I am writing
or creating, there are
no right or wrongs
here.

"

Date_____/_____/_____

Am I done yet?

I am a wife and mother of five. As if my life isn't already hectic enough, I had the nerve to have five children under the age of 6. A kindergarten student, a preschooler, one that potty training, one learning to walk and talk and a newborn.

On top of the children my husband is a Pentecostal preacher who teaches bible study on Tuesday nights and Sunday school and occasional Sunday morning service. I wake early in the morning to look after the affairs of the house. On a good day I get to sleep in until 8am. I clean and make breakfast, or I make breakfast while I am cleaning. I must play with the kids

From The Authors Pen

This was an incomplete piece that I found in my journal. It was raw and real. So real it seems was interrupted by something that caused me not to finish. If you know me, you know that we added three more the five moving from #5Kids2Arms to #MoreKidsThanArms. I can remember that my life was a joy and a daunting task all at once. The oldest was in Kindergarten and now he is a high school graduate and I have five teenagers in my house which is an entirely different type of daunting. WE have grown and experienced so much over the years; With the kids, in life, in marriage. Life has dealt us its share of pain and obstacles, but the thing I hold tight to is that we have done it together.

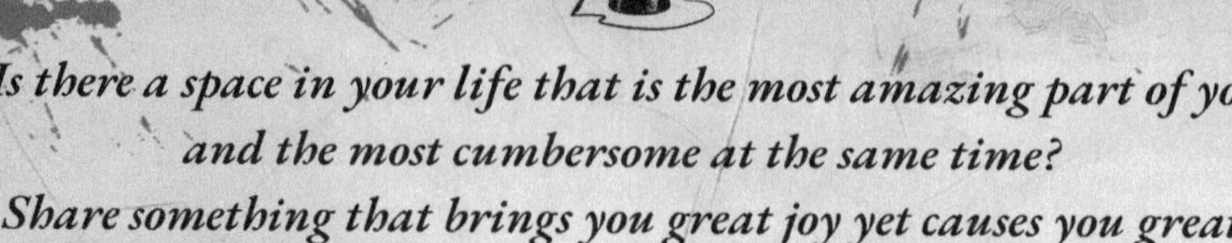

Is there a space in your life that is the most amazing part of you and the most cumbersome at the same time?
Share something that brings you great joy yet causes you great sacrifice at the same time.

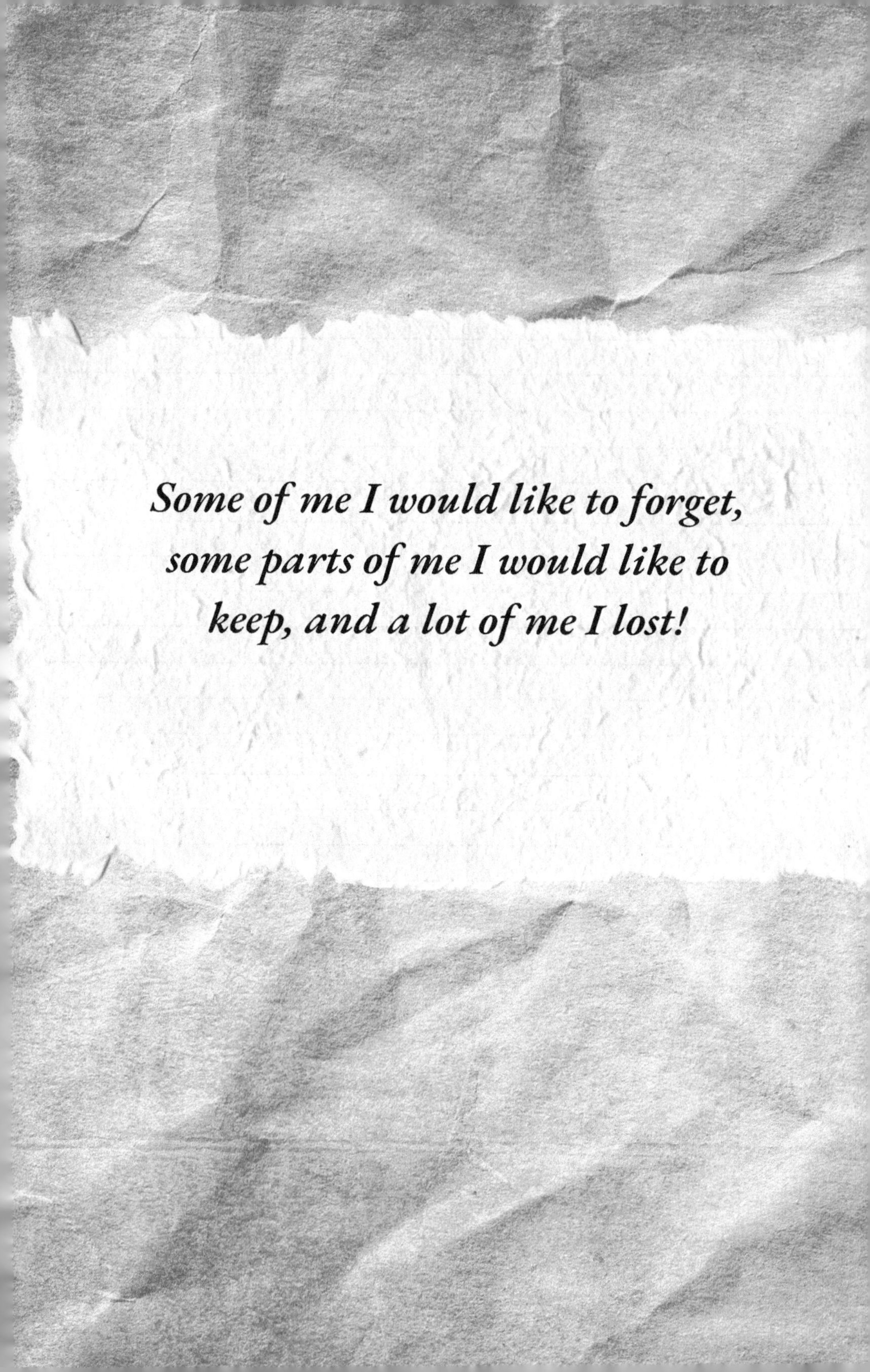
Some of me I would like to forget,
some parts of me I would like to
keep, and a lot of me I lost!

From The Authors Pen

I have shared a few times that I found these half written, incomplete heavy sentences in some of my journals. This is one of those entries that I was only able to muster but one sentence. However, as I read this sentence its loaded. I did not all a date to this sentence, but I can think back to a time where I felt like I was not present. I would look into the mirror, and I did not recognize who was staring back at me. I was lost in wife, mother, minister, daughter, sister and friend. I was battling my own mental illness and trying to manage life without medication. I was exhausted and depressed but still moving along as if all was well. I was everything for everyone but could not find the true pieces of myself. It has taken a lot therapy and self-work to get to the place I am told. I am found what I thought was lost right there inside of me. I just needed to give her the permission to live and live her truth.

Be honest about what hurt and what uncomfortable about life. I had to say to myself it okay to return to you; I know how to handle you now. I will be better to you; I will invest in you like I do everything else. And ultimate I felt safe enough to return to myself.

All that is lost can be found... I shared my experience of losing myself. It was hard work to return to myself and live the life I knew I deserved. So I ask you think about the lost in your life something you want back maybe it's joy or peace or freedom. Maybe like me it's the self you love but lost because you gave yourself away to other things. Journal about the lost and journey back.

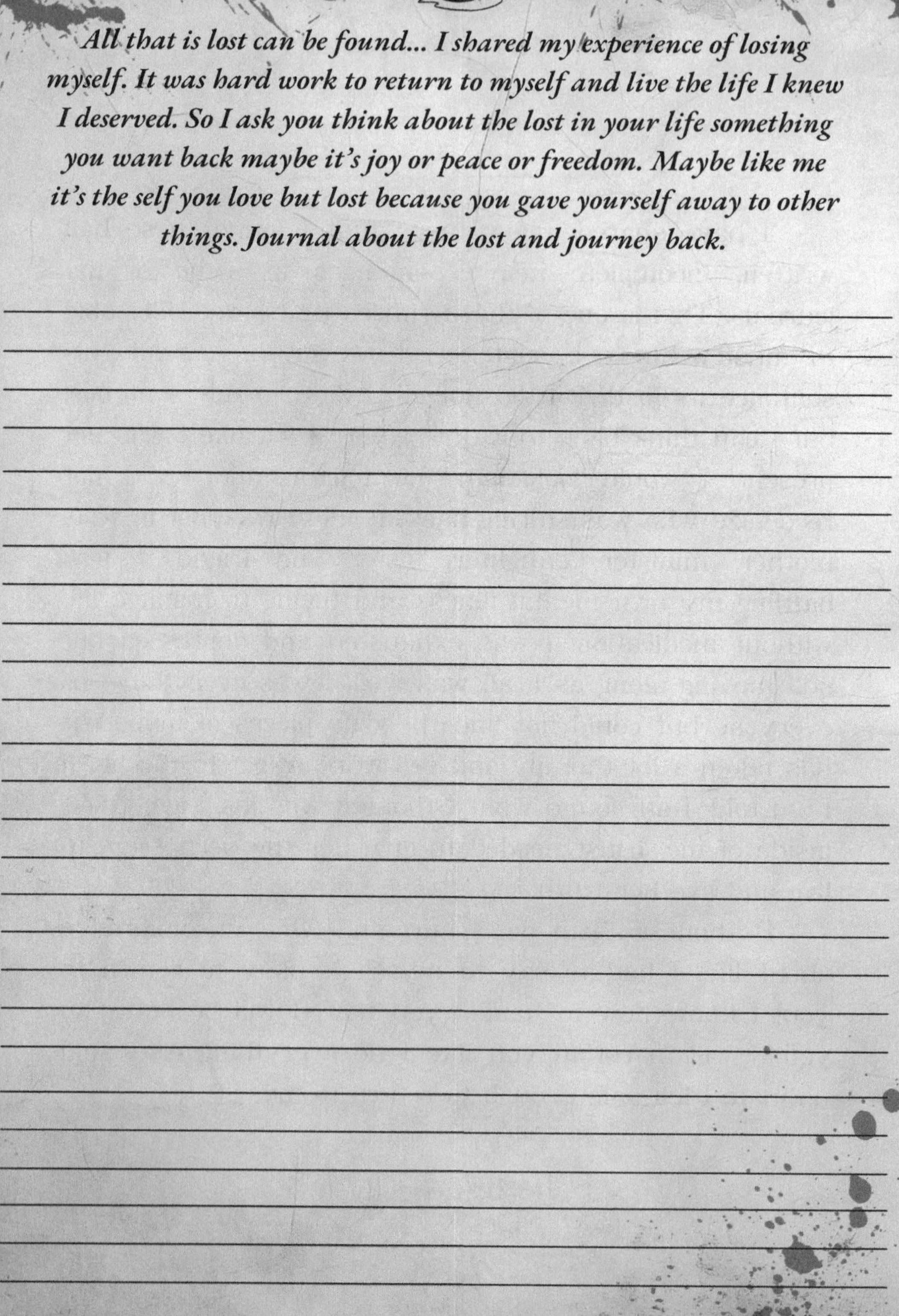

Birth of a Writer

Since becoming a mother I have learned five times over that giving birth is not easy. The labor is long and steady at first, causing some mild discomfort, but ever more intensifying as you get closer to your expected end.

As you travail, you must remember to keep calm and make your breathing steady so you can make it there. I now know that writers are born just about the same way. You learn the joy that you can feel when looking at those lines in front of you as they fill page after page.

Sometimes, you are tired and sick to your stomach, but you keep writing. And then after a while, the pains and the discomforts come in. Life begins to happen. You lose friends, your families turn their backs and all for what? To birth something out of you.

Being birthed is a tight squeeze. It seems long, dark, and hard, but there is always light on the other side. At this time when the Lord has commissioned me to be a great writer, I feel the most discomfort.

When people call me names or critics say I have gotten "soft",. I must remember that it's God who called me, it's God who chose this life for me. I must remember that between the lines is where I must find my comfort and know at the end of the journey is something great, something more precious than I can expect. It is the birth of a true writer.

This is your space to write freely.
Give birth to the unwritten thoughts within.

"Being birthed is a tight squeeze. It seems long, dark, and hard, but there is always light on the other side!"

Date____/____/____

Grateful

So many times, we diagnose our days before they begin, We put things into play with our lips. We unlace God's shoes and force him into the passenger seat with our controlling selves. And as soon as we get into the traffic jams of life or we are given a ticket too big for our bank account, we relinquish the keys and say, "Okay your turn now!"

Today at this very moment, I give all my control to God. I say no more me but all of you. I will let my lips breath life and my thoughts be gardens for positive thoughts, Free of the weeds the enemy can plant. Weeds that choke the life out of the vision and promises that God has given me.

Grateful doesn't mean that everything went your way, Grateful is more of an accessory than it is an outfit. Grateful is an option, but when worn makes the outfit all the more beautiful!

From The Authors Pen

We are taught gratitude at a young age, as our mother handed us a cookie, or gave us some juice; I can hear my mother say "what do you say?"

As believers we are taught that gratitude is a firm principle, just be thankful for what you have. No matter how things are just be grateful. Over the years, I have learned to be grateful for the little that I have or what chaos is my life, because someone somewhere would gladly exchange a little bit of this crazy I have in my life!

Sometimes it helps to take a breath and forget about what was causing stress and focus on what is good about life. I admonish you today to write a few lines about what it is that you are grateful for Think on the good!

Home to be Thankful For

I guess the very first thing to be thankful for is the fact that I have a home and a family that gives it life. My children add the personality to my home that makes it cozy. I am also that in a time of recession I am able to be a stay at home mom and enjoy the luxury of life. The greatest is that my children are all healthy and able to make a mess. None of them are sick or bedridden. Bless the name of God that I am not cleaning a hospital room.

I think that it's a blessing that in my husband's heart of hearts he sincerely wants me to be home so that his children are monitored and we buffer the enemy that way. Another thing to be thankful for is that I am the envy of all the other moms and dads alike. There are many things I can complain about not having enough time to clean, too much house to clean, and always having to clean but I am thankful that I am able to clean. Able to maintain my home in the way I see fit. There is so much to thank God for!

From The Authors Pen

At one point in my life, I do not think that I was thankful for the home or the life I had, the truth be told I was often depressed and overwork feeling like I was living someone else's life. At the time of writing this entry my kids were young and running around; three of them were diapers. My husband and I seemed to always be busy, we were broke and exhausted with no end in sight.

At the time of writing this entry my kids were young, they were running around and three of them were in diapers. My husband and I seemed to always be busy and often exhausted with no end. Then one day I met a lady who told me that she had been pregnant 12 times and each time the lord had not seemed fit for those babies to be born. She was watching me breastfeed my baby and pin the toddler down with my leg and she smiled at me which sparked our conversation. When I heard her story I suddenly was grateful for the blessing I was taking for granted.

What are you grateful for?
Have you had an encounter that made you look at your situation differently and suddenly know that you were blessed whether you believed it or not ? Write about that time...

“There is so much to thank God for!”

Date____/____/____

As a black woman in this world, there are subtleties that tell you that you aren't enough. That you don't belong, and your voice doesn't matter.... I say to you that everything about you matters, you deserve to be in any space you find yourself in.

Have you ever felt like you did not belong or that you simply were not enough?

Write about that time ...

"... you deserve to be in any space you find yourself in!"

Date____/____/____

Letter to my FAMU Self

Dear Talethia,

If you could see yourself now, life didn't turn out exactly the way you had planned it ten years ago. Actually, its quite different.

If only you could learn is that things aren't what they always seem and sometimes getting what's deep in your heart is better than having come true those surface things that will make you something to the world. When I got to Florida A&M I was young and fresh. The world had endless possibilities. I was parent less and free to do as please while trying to get an education at the same because "I had dreams", " I wanted to change the world"!

Life quickly taught me some lessons. There was a price to pay for being grown and on your own. The reality of being a first-generation college student and having to "make it" so that your success could in some way inspire or finance your families' dreams is way too much for one to bare. You would soon learn this in a harsh lesson.

Listen to this part and listen well girl because if you are ever to avoid this experience again you are going to have to hear me. The year that you "lost your mind" for a lack of better words was more about freeing your mind than it was about paralyzing it. The hallucinations and delusions were all to open your mind to teach you how to trust yourself.

Letter to my FAMU Self

When everyone thought you were crazy, you may have been; crazy very crazy about you. This time afforded you the opportunity to spend time with the real you. Not the you everyone knew and loved, but the you that was a stranger to herself. The girl who had hopes and dreams far more sentimental than the halls of the supreme court and deeper than the black of a judge's robe, but so deep they were hidden from you.

Don't let anyone make you feel bad about this time in your life, embrace it. Hug it, Love it, Hang on to it. Because it was this time that you found you. Don't get too comfortable girl and stay there because although being "crazy" was world wind finding out you were pregnant at the end of that year will change the entire trajectory of your life.

We have learned so much and grown so much, I know you would be proud. Now you carry on because you will soon discover that FAMU literally supplies you with what you need to discover yourself, take chances and ultimately gain the desires of your heart that you did not know you had.

Shine On Girl,

Talethia D. Edwards

From The Authors Pen

Growing up under pressure in Miami, Florida, I was never meant to make it out of that place. I was born the oldest to a strong woman, who did not always say things just right but she gave us what she had. I came to FAMU attempting to escape a place. A place that was familiar but that didn't quite seem or feel like home to me. I was looking for newness, I was trying to find myself. I wanted more out of life. I am young , footloose and fancy free. I thought I knew what I wanted out of life, I thought I knew where I was going but college took me on a roller coaster more than a journey. I found myself alright, I found more than I was bargaining for. I found out what heredity actually meant. Life can be funny that way because I lost my mind, had a baby, and was married all within a year.

All of the years of pressure and trying to hold it all together it all came crashing down on me. This time was a moment in my life where all roads began to come together: the place where I was running from, the place I was running to and where I would ultimately end up.

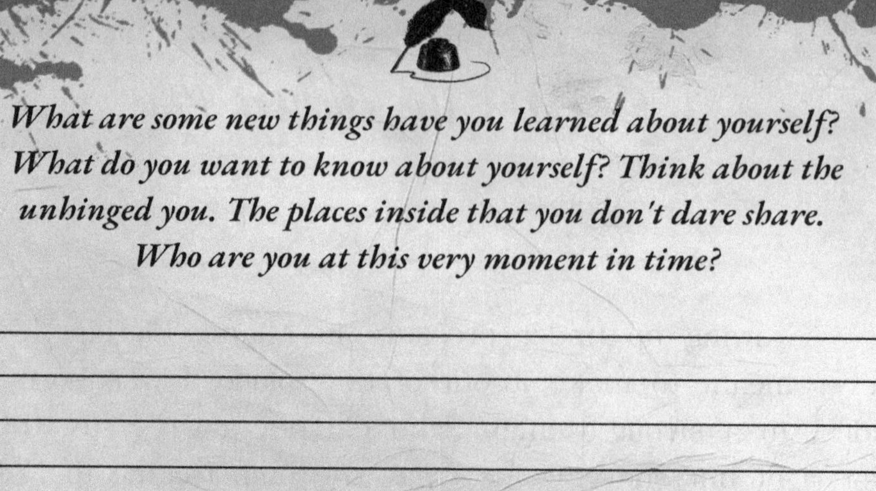

What are some new things have you learned about yourself? What do you want to know about yourself? Think about the unhinged you. The places inside that you don't dare share. Who are you at this very moment in time?

"Don't let anyone make you feel bad about this time in your life, embrace it. Hug it. Love it. Hang on to it!"

Date____/____/____

Free to Release

I struggled for a long time to write these words down, to put them in a book. While I talked a lot I didn't quite know if anyone had been listening. As I watched the world get louder and louder around me, I began to feel surely there was not much I could say that would penetrate the world and stick in time. I was confident and skeptical all at the same time. I watched each new year pass me by without the words on paper. Just a thought in my head and a desire in my heart. But not this time. Here I am writing these words, approaching a new year and ready to release them into the world. A sacrifice of my privacy and myself so that I am free, free to release and create and move on pass this time in life to something new.

This is your space to write down anything in or on your mind !

New Year Thoughts

HAPPY NEW YEAR

The daydreams of where I am going cloud the view of the red flag life is waving trying to get me to pay attention. Today, I listen to myself.

Life is more than the everyday routines we deem so important; it's about praying for people we don't know, and wishing well to the disliked.

This morning, words pinging the walls of my brain, screaming for me to capture them in time. Write me down, write me down. Write me down, cry my thoughts. Don't let me get lost.

Sometimes things are short and choppy and they feel very incomplete, but when you take a look back, you realize just how complete it was in that moment. This entry was probably interrupted by whatever could have been going on in my life at the time, but reading it today, it is fitting.

So many times I have been in this place of hoping and wishing for myself, only dreaming of where and what I wanted to be doing, but today I live out loud, walking out the plan and will of God for my life without apology because I know now that it's important to actually do what has been in my head and heart and what feel right to my soul.

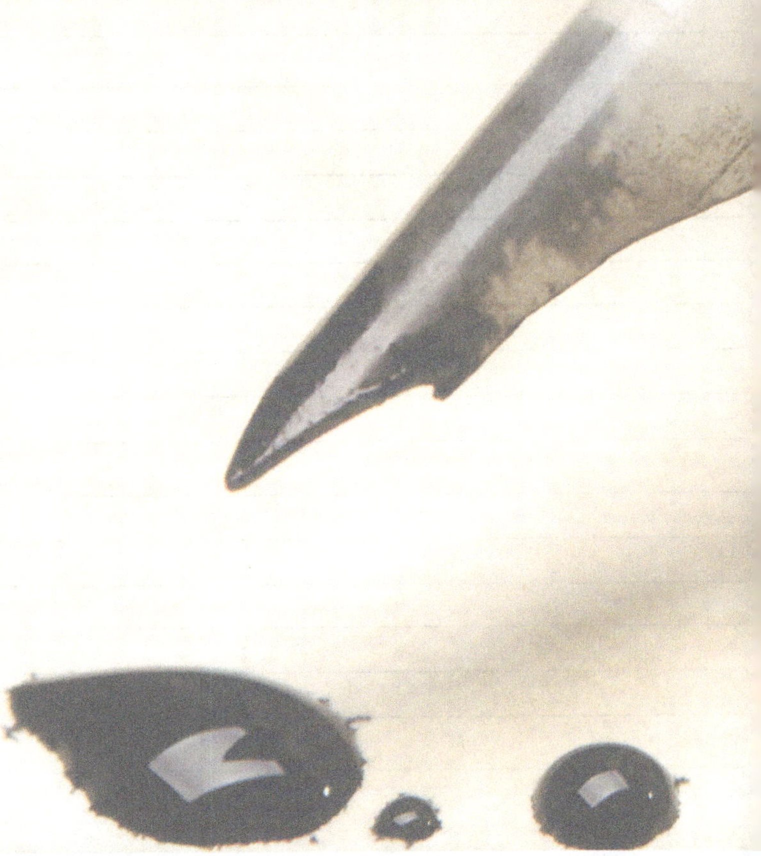

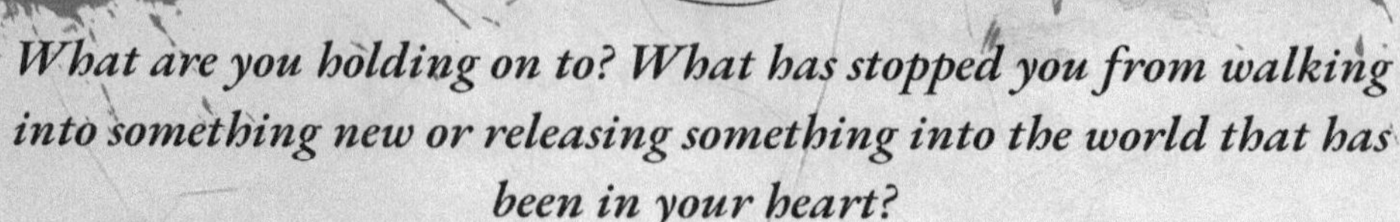

What are you holding on to? What has stopped you from walking into something new or releasing something into the world that has been in your heart?

I encourage you today... Write those things down as we go into the new year, think about what fences you have to tear down, what permissions you have to give yourself.

List them here and then let them go...

“

Today, I listen to myself.
Life is more than the everyday routines we deem so important!

”

Date_____/_____/_____

Good morning.
Today I say hello to dreams and possibilities, I dance to the rhyme of the motivation in my head, hearing only, 'You can do it! as I enjoyed the tunes of untapped potential.

Think about a place in your life that you were unsure of. You may have been living the life that was being dealt to you, but it was a place that you felt you wanted more, you deserved more and were looking for more out of life. Maybe you are still in that place of flux and wishing to live the life that you dream about on the vision board you have created. Write about what's next for you? How can you begin to live the dream in your head and heart? Feel free to make a list or name people that can help.

"...say hello to dreams and possibilities!"

Date____/____/____

2/2/22

I have seen these numbers almost all my life and never knew what they meant. I claimed them as my number. I used them to identify myself back in the days when we had beepers.

I am writing today not just to be obedient but I am writing to be free. I have had a strange relationship with paper because it understands all of me. It held the things I couldn't, but somewhere along the way I stopped writing, I learned how to push down. I learned how to block, how to feel only what I wanted to. The freedom that I am writing for not only for me but for my children. It's for my family, it's for the generations to come.

I am not sure what God is going to do, but I am going to write and share whatever he gives me.

What numbers, signs, or scriptures have you been seeing lately and what do you believe they mean for you?

"

I am not sure what God is going to do, but I am going to write and share whatever he gives me!

"

Date____/____/____

Thoughts On The Road

Sometimes it's surprising what the open road can do for your thoughts. It can open your brain and your heart. Too many times, I find myself closed up. Closed up to my thoughts, the people around me and the situations I am placed in. That's not a good place to be.

Enjoying the company of my husband, with not much to do but be into each other, I realize we allow things to cloud our space therefore we close each other off. My advice today is making sure you get away. Whether it's just a getaway to a town over or a well thought out vacation, you need the time to do nothing at all but remind each other of how and when you fell in love and how much you love each other.

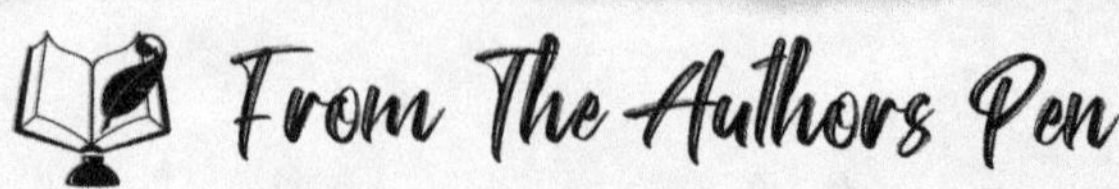

The road for me is a place of peace and solace; as a child my mother would put me in the car and take me on rides when she wanted me to fall asleep.

I grew up loving taking rides in the car, no matter who was driving or where they were going, I wanted to go. Today is no different, I am married and my husband is the primary driver and many times while we are on the road I am trying to be quiet and listen to my own thoughts, or pray or as my mother conditioned me to do... fall asleep. But sometimes I am in the car and I am wanting to find closeness with my husband because with the hustle and bustle of our lives we can find ourselves missing each other.

Do you like taking long drives, or are you a rider on the long drive? What are you usually doing on that drive? What's on your mind? I want to invite you to write down the perfect drive for you... what do you want from the trip? Is there some music from your past that you want to blast or a podcast you've been wanting to check out? Jot it down here and keep it in mind for the next trip.

"Sometimes it's surprising what the open road can do for your thoughts. It can open your brain and your heart."

Date____/____/____

2/4/22

Why am I still stalling?
I am brilliant, what I have to say is brilliant, it's bold and it's beautiful of me! It's me that the world is waiting on. So many people are waiting and hoping someone will be bold enough to share a story that would reflect them and their place.

I have hesitated and stalled on many things in my life. The lesson in the previous entry is one in retrospect. sometimes you must live and or do to give others permission to do the same.

What causes you to procrastinate or What negative self talk keeps you stalling?

"It's me that the world is waiting on!"

Date____/____/____

He's Talking To Me

Who?
Me?
Him?
Oh, me?
Are you sure about that?
Do you know who I am?
Do you know where I have been and what I have done?
You can't be talking to me.

Me?
Nah, couldn't be.
I have an idea of things like that but ... Do what?
I don't think I can, not smart enough, not savvy enough, not rich enough.
You can't be talking to me.

Oh, really so you believe I am equipped for a task such as that?.
Your faith in me is a little too great.
You must not know who you are talking to.
My lineage says I can't, no one from where I am from has ever done that.
You can't be talking to me.

Say what?
I am fearfully and wonderfully made, you created me in your likeness.
Equipped me with your spirit?
Made for you and by you and for your glory.
All these things are me?
What, YOU believe in me?
Then finally I know YOU must be talking to me.

From The Authors Pen

I don't know about you, but I have many dialogues with God. It's mostly God trying to convince me of how he sees me, and of course I cannot believe him because most of it goes totally against what my upbringing or current situation is saying.

I am almost always in disbelief, you have just taken a peek in a one-sided conversation I was having with God.

What are your conversations like with God?

"I am fearfully and wonderfully made, you created me in your likeness."

Date_____/_____/_____

I don't want scraps, I'm not mad, but I want off the merry go round. I have to learn to see things for what they actually are, and stop fooling myself. I get it. At this point I am fragile, I understand that about myself. I want to be whole, and I want to be loved with trueness. Everything in my life has felt false, and I have to be the one to change that. I am tired of being hurt, ignored, blamed, ridiculed.

Enough of Talethia as the door mat because she is strong, long suffering, kind-hearted, generous or whatever word people tell themselves to make it okay to use me, ignore me and damage me.

No one has ever stood up and protected me, I am making a stand to do that for me this time. I watch the patterns of people all around me, and what I am told. Pray! Well, I am praying up off my knees with my back firm.

Thank you, but no thank you.

What are you tired of and ready to change today?

“

I am
praying up off
my knees with
my back firm.

”

Date____/____/____

2/8/22

Every day I am learning more and more how to trust God. How to be okay with who I am, how to be appreciative and thankful for the roads I have traveled down. This weekend I was able to participate in a read in. It's culturally an appropriate event for the black History Month celebration. I read some inspiring words from Toni Morrison's book that she left us when she died.

I stood there reading her words on the page, thinking, 'Will someone ever read my words, will I be bold enough like Toni or Maya to share with the world what the lord has given me. Does any of this really make sense?'At this moment, none of it makes sense to me. I am just doing it as an act of obedience. I want to get to the next level. I fuss with Harold about circling the drain but what am I doing... circling the drain making excuses.

I can remember when I was young I had all of these great dreams to actually become the first African American woman Supreme Court justice and had all of these ideas of what it would take for me to get to that place, and I vividly remember saying that at the end of the day all I really wanted to be was a great writer. I enjoy the time I spend with paper or my screen now. Sharing all of the deep thoughts and innermost secrets. I learn to peel back the layers here. I learn to be all that I am not.

I learn to be honest and transparent, broken or confident. I learn that what the world thinks of me doesn't matter, and all that matters is what the lord says I am and what I believe. I can leave it all on the table. Take the mask off, relieve myself of the many hats or the plates I am juggling. I don't have to know, I just have to be. oh how good that feels just to be.

Have you ever thought about what it means to actually just be... still, calm, quiet.... With nothing pulling on you or demanding your time?

2/8/22

I feel time stops when I am here with you... writing and sharing.

Since I started this, I have been trying to find the genesis of it all. When did my love affair with paper begin? Who introduced us? I can't remember.. well I vaguely remember my first journal/ notebook. There was a little ballerina on the front. It was purple and pink kind of hazy. I opened it and shared it with myself. An intimate experience I would fall in love with. One that would save my life, honestly.

I might have lost my mind long before I did if I hadn't found out that only paper would understand all the intricate parts of me. I might have been depressed if I didn't have paper to help me navigate adolescence.

I am here.. we are here, and learning to get acquainted again.. learning how to just be with each other. It feels good and it feels right. To be here with you... only paper understands.

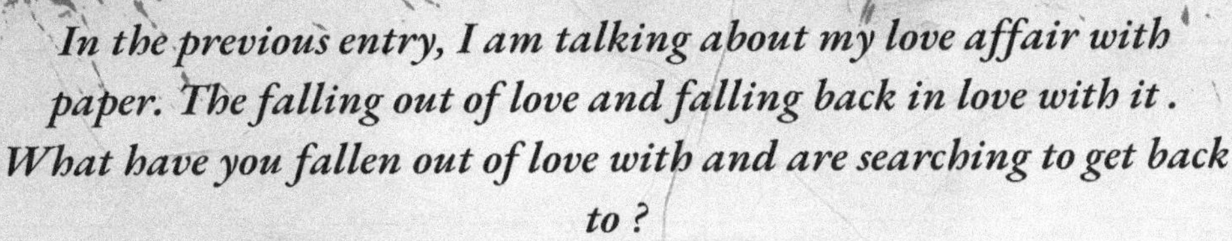

In the previous entry, I am talking about my love affair with paper. The falling out of love and falling back in love with it . What have you fallen out of love with and are searching to get back to ?

"I might have lost my mind long before I did if I hadn't found out that only paper would understand all the intricate parts of me."

Date____/____/____

All that I can do and be and say... it's already inside of me. I am complete.

What do you need to be complete ?

What holds you back from being complete ?

"Who I am, and all that I am, only paper understands."

Made in the USA
Columbia, SC
05 April 2025

56006670R30083